MELBOURNE

THE CITY AT A

C000262820

Southern Cross Stati
The undulating wave-l
striking aspect of the r
Street Station, which w
for the 2006 Commonw
Spencer Street/Collins

Melbourne Central
Kisho Kurokawa's 211m office tower, finished
in 1991, connects to a retail hub redeveloped
by Ashton Raggatt McDougall in 2005.
La Trobe Street/Swanston Street

Rialto Towers
These 252m steel-and-glass office blocks
were completed in 1986. Survey the city
from Vue de Monde (see p041) on Level 55.
525 Collins Street, T 9614 5888

Federation Square
This controversial development combines
groundbreaking architecture with arts and
leisure facilities on the banks of the Yarra.
See p014

Eureka Tower
Architects Fender Katsalidis' vertical city
has 92 floors and, at 297m, is one of the
tallest residential buildings in the world.
See p009

Crown Entertainment Complex
Melbourne's fun palace boasts three hotels
(see p024), a casino, restaurants, theatres,
bars, cinemas and a bowling lounge.
8 Whiteman Street, T 9292 8888

Kings Domain
Surrounding Government House, the Shrine
of Remembrance and the Sidney Myer
Music Bowl, this series of parks by the river
connects with the Royal Botanic Gardens.

INTRODUCTION
THE CHANGING FACE OF THE URBAN SCENE

Melbourne often tops most-liveable-city lists, much to the chagrin of Sydney. It can't compete physically, of course – the southern capital's landscape is flat, its beaches less than stunning – but looks aren't everything, and Melbourne is a goldmine for urban explorers. Nothing is obvious, and many of its delights are hidden. The city's evolution around a grid system has meant the lanes off the main roads offer a way for entrepreneurs to base businesses in the thick of it. Independent galleries, boutiques and even bathhouses are found in back alleys or up nondescript stairways. Often they have complex identities: a cocktail bar will display the work of local artists; a store that sells homewares serves a mean eggs Benedict.

The city's built history has been well preserved, and many of its contemporary architectural firms – Denton Corker Marshall, Wood/Marsh, ARM – are globally acclaimed, their fingerprints all over the skyline. Yet, away from the CBD, the suburbs retain a villagey vibe and provide an insight into Melbourne's multiple personalities. As well as boho Fitzroy, cosmopolitan Carlton, showy South Yarra and bayside St Kilda, other locales are emerging: Prahran and Windsor are known for their vintage stores and gastropubs; Collingwood and Brunswick are more edgy, but hip venues are opening apace.

When planning a visit, cast your eye over the cultural calendar. There's nothing Melbourne likes more than a festival. Oh, and did we mention the cuisine? That alone is reason to spend time here.

ESSENTIAL INFO

FACTS, FIGURES AND USEFUL ADDRESSES

TOURIST OFFICE
Federation Square
T 9658 9658
www.thatsmelbourne.com.au

TRANSPORT
Airport transfer to city centre
SkyBuses depart regularly. The journey takes 20 minutes and the fare is A$18
www.skybus.com.au
Car hire
Hertz
T 9663 6244
Public transport
T 180 080 0007
www.ptv.vic.gov.au
Trams are the best way to get around the city. They run from about 5am to 1am. You need a Myki Card to use public transport
Taxi
Silver Top Taxi
T 131 008
Cabs are easily hailed on the street

EMERGENCY SERVICES
Emergencies
T 000
Late-night pharmacy (until 12am)
Tambassis Pharmacy Brunswick
32 Sydney Road
T 9387 8830

CONSULATES
British Consulate-General
17th floor
90 Collins Street
T 9652 1600
www.gov.uk/government/world/australia
US Consulate-General
553 St Kilda Road
T 9526 5900
melbourne.usconsulate.gov

POSTAL SERVICES
Post office
Shop 1, 250 Elizabeth Street
T 131 318
Shipping
Pack & Send
452 Flinders Street
T 9620 2277

BOOKS
Capital: Melbourne When it Was the Capital City of Australia 1901-27 by Kristin Otto (Text Publishing)
Design City Melbourne by Leon van Schaik and John Gollings (Wiley)
The Melbourne Book: A History of Now by Maree Coote (MelbourneStyle)
Monkey Grip by Helen Garner (Penguin)

WEBSITES
Architecture
www.robinboyd.org.au
Newspaper
www.theage.com.au

EVENTS
Melbourne Festival
www.melbournefestival.com.au
Open House Melbourne
www.openhousemelbourne.org

COST OF LIVING
Taxi from Melbourne Airport to the CBD
A$70
Cappuccino
A$4.40
Packet of cigarettes
A$21
Daily newspaper
A$2.30
Bottle of champagne
A$90

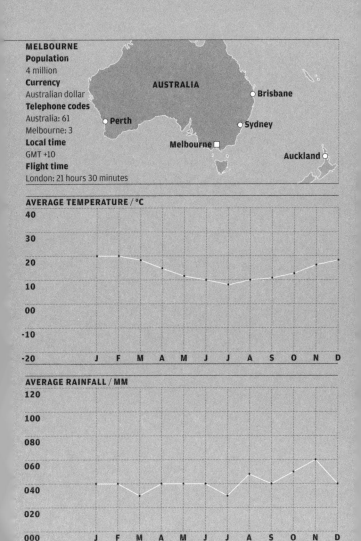

MELBOURNE
Population
4 million
Currency
Australian dollar
Telephone codes
Australia: 61
Melbourne: 3
Local time
GMT +10
Flight time
London: 21 hours 30 minutes

AUSTRALIA

○ Brisbane
○ Perth
○ Sydney
Melbourne □
Auckland ○

AVERAGE TEMPERATURE / °C

	J	F	M	A	M	J	J	A	S	O	N	D
40
30
20
00
-10
-20

AVERAGE RAINFALL / MM

	J	F	M	A	M	J	J	A	S	O	N	D
120
100
080
060
040
020
000

NEIGHBOURHOODS

THE AREAS YOU NEED TO KNOW AND WHY

To help you navigate the city, we've chosen the most interesting districts (see below and the map inside the back cover) and colour-coded our featured venues, according to their location; those venues that are outside these areas are not coloured.

CENTRAL BUSINESS DISTRICT

The CBD is not only Melbourne's business heart but also contains shopping, eating, drinking and arts establishments (see p036). Unlike similar areas in other towns, it never sleeps – the laneways are a hive of late-night activity (see p039). You can find everything you need here, although it would be a shame not to venture further, as Melbourne's trams run the length and breadth of the city and are easy to use.

SOUTHBANK

It might be just across the Yarra River from the CBD, but Southbank has a completely different feel. Densely developed, it's home to the huge Crown Complex, which includes the Metropol hotel (see p024) and Nobu (T 9292 7879), as well as the Arts Centre (100 St Kilda Road, T 130 018 2183), which hosts a Sunday crafts market. Tourists and locals alike come here to soak up both the views and the boulevard culture.

CARLTON

When Italian migrants flocked to the city after WWII, most put down roots around Carlton, so it's hard to find a bad espresso here. There are also great shops, such as Readings Books (309 Lygon Street, T 9347 6633), and a cinema. It is no longer the epicentre of Italian cuisine, but DOC (295 Drummond Street, T 9347 2998) serves authentic thin crispy pizzas, and local institution Brunetti (380 Lygon Street, T 9347 2801) makes irresistible pastries.

ST KILDA

For sun and sand – but unfortunately no surf – head to this perennially popular bayside suburb. There are two halves to the district: the rough-and-ready Fitzroy Street and the more genteel Acland Street, which has some superb Jewish patisseries. Down by the water are the pier, the St Kilda Sea Baths (10-18 Jacka Boulevard, T 9525 4888) and the Luna Park fairground (18 Lower Esplanade, T 9525 5033).

SOUTH YARRA

Parts of this neighbourhood feel like a quaint, exclusive village. South Yarra is within easy reach of the Royal Botanic Gardens and Fawkner Park, so it's also rather leafy and green. Smart shops and boutiques line Toorak Road and Chapel Street, and the restaurants in this area, including the intimate Sardinian Da Noi (95 Toorak Road, T 9866 5975), are some of the best in all of Melbourne.

COLLINGWOOD/FITZROY

This bohemian enclave has come alive in the past 10 years and its regeneration shows little evidence of abating. The main thoroughfare, Brunswick Street, is packed with indie cafés and shops. But it is the gems on Gertrude Street (see p034), like Cutler & Co (see p051), and, increasingly, Smith Street, which boasts a cluster of excellent new eateries – try Josie Bones (No 98, T 9417 1878) – that will delight those who are searching for the unique.

LANDMARKS
THE SHAPE OF THE CITY SKYLINE

Melbourne has been blessed with the patronage of great aesthetes since the first European settlers arrived in 1835. Grand mansions from that era survive, and trams and cars still travel along wide, tree-lined promenades. In more recent years, some of Australia's finest architects have made their mark on what would otherwise have been a very flat, rather ugly, city landscape.

Since the mid-1990s, Melbourne has instigated a programme to redevelop its cultural venues. Architect Mario Bellini oversaw a 2003 revamp of the National Gallery of Victoria (180 St Kilda Road, T 8620 2222) and an expansion of the MTC (see p066) was unveiled in 2009. An eye has also been trained on the past, and buildings such as the 1847 Como Historic House (Williams Road/Lechlade Avenue, T 9827 2500), now part of the National Trust of Australia's portfolio, have been preserved. Southbank and the CBD are filling up with thrusting skyscrapers – the tallest being the 297m Eureka Tower (7 Riverside Quay, T 9693 8888), designed by architects Fender Katsalidis and opened in 2006. The observation deck on Level 88 is a great place from which to get your bearings.

Interestingly, though, some of the city's most readily identified landmarks, such as the MCG (see p012) and AAMI Park (see p094), are the product of one of its major obsessions – sport. To gloss over them would be to ignore Melbourne's beating heart.

For full addresses, see Resources.

Melbourne Gateway

Denton Corker Marshall's bright, imposing sculpture welcomes you to the city on the way in from the airport. Fans of this local architectural firm will recognise its signature design marks — bold colours and abstract shapes — all over the project. Thirty-nine angled red beams on the north side form a guard of honour, while a 70m yellow beam (wags have nicknamed it the Cheesestick) is cantilevered across the Citylink tollway from the opposite side of the road. There's also a yellow metal sound tube that protects nearby housing from traffic noise. According to the architects: 'The beam acts as a symbolic archway, the urban equivalent of a boom gate in the up position. The result is a powerful and dynamic gesture that opens up the city to visitors.'
Citylink/Flemington Road

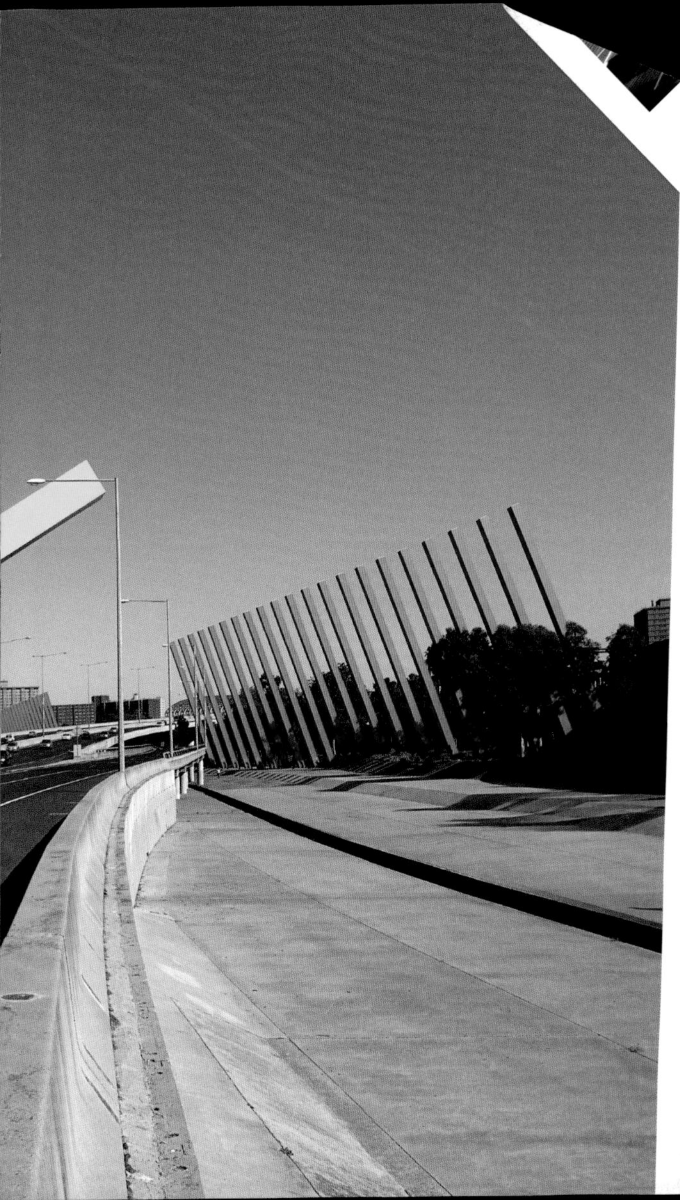

MCG

The state-of-the-art Melbourne Cricket Ground (MCG) is impressive on many levels. Not only is it the largest cricket stadium in the world, seating 95,000, but it is often full – proof, if it were needed, of the local love of sport. The first stand was built here in 1854 and the latest redevelopment, by Jackson Architecture, finished in 2006. The MCG is also used for Aussie Rules; up to 5,000 extra standing tickets are available for the AFL grand final in September. To ensure it is not damaged during the winter, the central cricket square is removed and dropped in at the start of each season. On non-event days, take a tour or visit the National Sports Museum (T 9657 8879), which has a cinema, interactive galleries and, scarily, a hologram of Shane Warne. *Yarra Park, Brunton Avenue, T 9657 8888, www.mcg.org.au*

Republic Tower

Erstwhile Victoria premier Jeff Kennett's privatisation programme led to a 1990s construction boom, and one of its major successes was this residential high-rise designed by architects Fender Katsalidis, completed in 2001. All sculptural concrete fins and dark glass, it comprises 36 storeys of apartments atop a five-level mixed-use podium. At street level there is a massive billboard known as the Republic Art Space, overseen by Tasmania's MONA Museum, on to which more than 30 artists from Australia and overseas, including Guo Jian, Julie Rrap and Polly Borland, have had their work displayed. In the background, distinguishable by its twin antennae, looms the tower of Melbourne Central, a mall and transport hub on the corner of La Trobe and Swanston Streets.
299 Queen Street, T 9670 7725

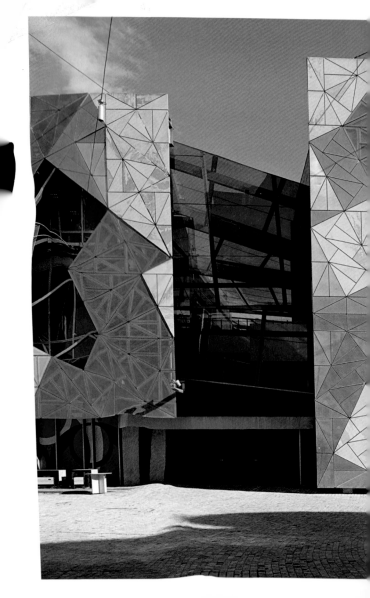

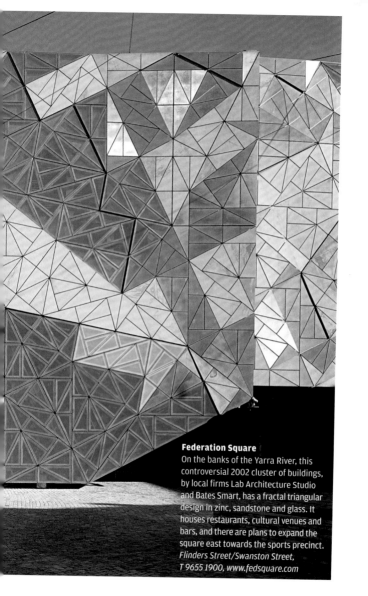

Federation Square
On the banks of the Yarra River, this controversial 2002 cluster of buildings, by local firms Lab Architecture Studio and Bates Smart, has a fractal triangular design in zinc, sandstone and glass. It houses restaurants, cultural venues and bars, and there are plans to expand the square east towards the sports precinct.
Flinders Street/Swanston Street, T 9655 1900, www.fedsquare.com

HOTELS

WHERE TO STAY AND WHICH ROOMS TO BOOK

Not surprisingly, Melbourne offers an excellent range of big-name hotels. The Sofitel (25 Collins Street, T 9653 0000) is impeccable and set in what is dubbed the Paris end of Collins Street, due to its leafy aspect and chichi boutiques. Also here is the Grand Hyatt (123 Collins Street, T 9657 1234), which has 546 luxe yet understated rooms – book a Grand View for stunning river vistas – and one of the city's best-kept secrets in its bar, RU-CO. Across the Yarra, The Langham (1 Southgate Avenue, T 8696 8888) is an opulent escape and, on floors 19 to 21, offers Club Terrace Rooms, each with a 50 sq m balcony and dining area. Further along the riverbank is the stylish Crown Metropol (see p024), the largest hotel in the country.

There is a fine choice of boutique dwellings. The Art Series Hotels, which include The Cullen (see p028), The Blackman (452 St Kilda Road, T 9039 1444) and The Olsen (637-641 Chapel Street, T 9040 1222), feature individual architecture and works by the Australian artist after whom each hotel is named. The Ovolo (see p020) has design aspects inspired by the street art of the laneways. In South Yarra, the sophisticated Lyall (16 Murphy Street, T 9868 8222) is favoured by the fashion set; we like Suite 401, which has two balconies. If you'd prefer to be near the beach, head to The Prince (opposite). Be aware that hotels fill up fast during sporting events, especially the Australian Open tennis and the Grand Prix. *For full addresses and room rates, see Resources.*

The Prince

This art deco pile has been at the heart of St Kilda life since 1940, and mixes urban chic with beachside cool (lighting fixtures are modified craypots). In 2011, local firm Meme Design refreshed the rooms, adding colour flashes and trinkets, like Jonathan Adler vases, to minimalist interiors, and reinvigorating the restaurant, Circa. The moody foyer (above) has just an Eames 'La Chaise' and a fabric wall hanging. We recommend Premier Suite 409 (overleaf) with its living area and balcony; some of the 39 rooms are on the small side. The Deck, which has an indoor pool, is a great spot for relaxing. Within the building you'll also find Mexican joint Acland St Cantina (T 9536 1175), gig venue Prince Bandroom (T 9536 1168) and Aurora Spa (see p088). *2 Acland Street, T 9536 1111, www.theprince.com.au*

Premier Suite 409, The Prince

Ovolo

Hong Kong firm Ovolo's first international hotel has a prime laneway location on the edge of Chinatown, near a multitude of restaurants and bars, and close to the designer stores on Collins Street. The 43 spacious rooms include 32 suites (some have two bedrooms and a kitchenette) with graphic splashes of colour, white-tiled bathrooms and bespoke artwork inspired by the area. There's individuality aplenty too. One Terrace Suite (503, opposite) has a punchbag and boxing gloves for letting off steam, and the Penthouse (501, above) comes with a pinball machine and an outdoor jacuzzi and daybeds. 'Grab'n'Go' Continental-style breakfast is offered in the lobby, but better value for money is the complimentary wi-fi and minibar. *19 Little Bourke Street, T 8692 0777, www.ovolohotels.com*

Middle Park Hotel

Local architects Six Degrees have taken
a masculine approach to appointments in
the 25 rooms (King Suite 108, right) in this
renovated pub – black mosaic bathrooms,
photos by Rennie Ellis (noted for capturing
the city's underbelly) and spare furnishings
finished with marble and leather – while
retaining many of the property's original
art deco features. There are the extras too:
Polaroid cameras, Kevin Murphy toiletries
and a minibar stocked with local goodies.
Downstairs has been spruced up but still
has the air of an authentic boozer, and
the dining room is overseen by Irish chef
Stephen Burke. There are proper fry-ups
for breakfast and excellent steaks and
Wagyu burgers for lunch and dinner. The
hotel is located a block from Albert Park.
102 Canterbury Road, T 9690 1958,
www.middleparkhotel.com.au

Crown Metropol

As soon as you enter the lobby (above) to see Korean artist Jae-Hyo Lee's sculptural chestnut wood spheres and the bell staff's hip uniforms you know that you're in for something unique. This is the latest funky offering at Southbank (it's linked to the luxe Crown Towers and restrained Crown Promenade), where 658 rooms boast floor-to-ceiling windows to take in the superb views. Facilities are impressive, including the top-floor pool (see p089) and the French-inspired Mr Hive Kitchen & Bar (T 9292 8300). Architects Bates Smart added a twist to the contemporary design by introducing retro-inspired pieces. Opt for a large City Luxe King room overlooking the skyline, or one of the Lofts, which have a living and dining area and huge tubs. *Level 1, 8 Whiteman Street, T 9292 6211, www.crownmetropol.com.au*

The Rialto

Born out of the refurb of two heritage-listed buildings – the neo-Gothic Rialto and Romanesque-style Winfield – The Rialto connected them with a soaring glass atrium (above), home to the Alluvial Restaurant and Bluestone Wine Lounge. The hotel oozes low-key sophistication. Its 253 Joseph Pang-designed rooms are decorated in shades of champagne and chocolate, with prints of the city on the walls. Most luxurious are the two Turret Suites (overleaf) – one has the bed in the turret, the other a claw-foot bath. Catch some rays on the wood-panelled deck by the indoor pool, dine at Italian chef Guy Grossi's Merchant restaurant (T 9614 7688) and try out the holistic treatments at the bijou East Day Spa (T 9620 5992). *495 Collins Street, T 8627 1400, www.ihg.com/hotels*

Turret Suite, The Rialto

The Cullen

Adam Cullen was a provocateur of the
Australian art scene (he died in 2012), so
when Art Series Hotels revealed that his
work would be shown in its first property
in Melbourne, eyebrows were raised.
The pieces scattered throughout, however,
aren't among his most controversial. The
rooms feature contemporary furniture
and kitchenettes, and the beds are so
comfy it's hard to drag yourself out of
them. Either book a Studio Suite (above),
the two-bed Cullen Suite (opposite) or one
of the 18 Deluxe Balcony Suites, so named
for their lime-and-black protruding 'pods'
that give the hotel facade, designed by
Jackson Clements Burrows, a clever visual
kick. The vibe of the neighbourhood suits
the mood of the hotel: Prahran is laidback
but still edgy, and there is a gaggle of
hip bars, clubs, cafés and shops nearby.
164 Commercial Road, T 9098 1555,
www.artserieshotels.com.au/cullen

Brooklyn Arts Hotel
Owner Maggie Fooke is a real presence
in her rambling 1865 mansion, and she
is keen to attract guests who have an
artistic background. The seven rooms
and common areas in this B&B near
Gertrude Street (see p034) are hung
with an eclectic collection of paintings
and photographs. Colour reigns, bibelots
abound and two Labradors greet visitors.
Book one of the two large rooms with
private bathrooms, lounges and high
ceilings – the Green Piano Room (left)
has its own joanna. When the weather's
warm, take your Continental breakfast
in the leafy courtyard. The Brooklyn won't
be to everyone's taste but it's excellent
value, has bags of personality and is
in easy strolling distance of some of the
city's most interesting neighbourhoods.
48-50 George Street, T 9419 9328,
www.brooklynartshotel.com.au

24 HOURS

SEE THE BEST OF THE CITY IN JUST ONE DAY

Melbourne delivers on three of the most important aspects of a city destination – cuisine, culture and retail. The trick to getting around smoothly is to make use of the tram system (the 112 travels to Brunswick Street in Fitzroy; the 86 from Gertrude Street to the centre; the free 35 takes a tourist circuit through the CBD), and the city is also kind to bike riders, due to its flat roads and plentiful lanes. Hire a retro machine from The Humble Vintage (T 043 203 2450) and pick it up from depots in the centre, St Kilda or Fitzroy.

Collingwood is your first stop for breakfast, at CIBI (opposite). The Compound Interest: Centre for the Applied Arts (15-25 Keele Street, T 8060 9745) is nearby and houses galleries, small presses and design outlets. Stroll through the back streets, taking in the Centre for Contemporary Photography (404 George Street, T 9417 1549), designed by Sean Godsell, and get a retail fix on Gertrude Street (see p034). After lunch at Jimmy Grants (see p035), head into the CBD to the galleries of Flinders Lane (see p036), and the Australian art, including fine Aboriginal and Torres Strait Islander work, at The Ian Potter Centre: NGV Australia (Federation Square, T 8620 2222). Have a sundowner round the corner at Riverland (Vaults 1–9, Federation Wharf, T 9662 1771) before dinner at Coda (see p038). In this city the night never finishes with dessert – the laneways (see p039) hold a legion of tiny bars and hip spaces. *For full addresses, see Resources.*

10.00 CIBI

Located off gentrifying Smith Street, this café/homewares store provides a taste of Japan. The dining area has raw wooden tables and mismatched chairs restored by owner Zenta Tanaka, and walls are hung with fabrics by Florence Broadhurst. The prep area is built from the floorboards of an old gym, the court markings no longer meeting up, in contrast to the ethos of the kitchen, where the philosophy is balanced and seasonal. During the week, breakfast is Western but on weekends the dishes turn Japanese – miso, grilled salmon, rice, omelette and green tea. To the rear of the warehouse, browse the artisanal ceramics, glassware and stationery. We were drawn to Masahiro Mori's porcelain cups and Sori Yanagi's stainless-steel kettles.

45 Keele Street, T 9077 3941,
www.cibi.com.au

11.30 Gertrude Street

This once seedy neighbourhood has been transformed into a sleek retail and eating strip. Head to Spacecraft (T 9486 0010) for screenprinted textiles; ESS (T 9495 6112) for structured silhouettes for men and women; Amor y Locura (T 9486 0270) for architectural antiques and Mexican folk art; and Title (T 9417 4477), a specialist book, CD and DVD store. Melbourne firm Crumpler (T 9417 5338) has gone global with its messenger bags, and the original store is located on the corner of Smith Street. Or get lost for hours at Tarlo & Graham (above; T 9417 7773), a haven for industrial pieces, scientific curios, tribal art and medical antiques. On a recent visit, we were taken by the vintage abacuses, German ships' lamps and a modernist stainless-steel tea set. The taxidermy crocodile, however, was a step too far.

13.00 Jimmy Grants

The humble souvlaki has gone upmarket at this Fitzroy joint co-owned by *MasterChef Australia* judge George Calombaris. The name of the casual no-bookings restaurant is a historical play on the word 'immigrants' and the brick walls are decorated with street artist Dan Wenn's huge paintings of a DC-3 and the Patris, a ship that brought workers from Europe. It's also the name of one of the best souvas in town – a light, fluffy pitta wrapped around fried prawns, cucumber, mint, coriander, honey and mayonnaise. Take a seat at one of the low tables or the bar, order a wrap with a grain salad and a Mythos Hellenic lager. It's open until 10pm. Nearby Po'Boy Quarter (T 9419 2130) serves up some of the finest gumbo and catfish rolls outside New Orleans. *113 Saint David Street, T 9416 0060, www.jimmygrants.com.au*

15.00 Flinders Lane

Once the heart of the rag trade, this long central street is lined with shops, cafés and galleries, some located either up or down stairwells, so keep your eyes peeled. At the eastern end, Craft (T 9650 7775) shows works by artists and designers such as Lucas Grogan and Anna Davern ('Fresh!' annual graduate exhibition, above), and has a fascinating store filled with jewellery, ceramics and textiles. Nearby is the Anna Schwartz Gallery (T 9654 6131). Worth exploring too is the Chicago-style Nicholas Building on the corner of Swanston Street. Its nine floors house unusual shops, such as poetry bookstore Collected Works, pop-ups and studios. Not all of the art in this part of the CBD is contained within four walls. The excellent outdoor graffiti galleries in Hosier Lane and Centre Place are an ever-changing part of the cityscape.

19.30 Coda

It opened in 2009 but there is still a buzz about this place. Co-owner Adam D'Sylva is one of the city's most exciting chefs, and his partners, Mykal and Kate Bartholomew, have run some of Melbourne's best floors. In this restaurant (above) and drinking den you're welcome to simply hang at the bar (opposite). The menu comprises European and Asian tasting plates; try the blackened quail, daikon and shiso salad, and roast duck yellow curry. The design by Projects of Imagination features custom-made basket lights and elicits a moody, sexy vibe. Afterwards, explore the laneways. Try Section 8 (T 043 029 1588), a space built from shipping containers and pallets, Bar Ampére (see p044), New Guernica (see p052) or rockin' Cherry Bar (T 9639 8122). *Basement, 141 Flinders Lane, T 9650 3155, www.codarestaurant.com.au*

URBAN LIFE

CAFÉS, RESTAURANTS, BARS AND NIGHTCLUBS

A night out in Melbourne could transport you in myriad directions. Splash out at Attica (74 Glen Eira Road, T 9530 0111), recognised as one of the world's best restaurants, where chef Ben Shewry's eight-course tasting menu with wine costs A$305. Martinis are a speciality at Gin Palace (10 Russell Place, T 9654 0533), and dancing carries on until dawn at Prahran's Boutique (134 Greville Street, T 9525 2322) at weekends. Trawl neighbourhood strips such as Smith Street in Collingwood, or Sydney Road in Brunswick, for cheap, ethnic eateries and quirky bars that push on into the early hours. The laneways hold plenty of gems, such as Von Haus (1a Crossley Street, T 9662 2756), which has a communal table, a great wine list and distressed walls; cocktail joint Murmur (Level 1, 17 Warburton Lane, T 9640 0395); and New Guernica (see p052).

Perhaps one of Melbourne's great after-dark strengths is its live music scene. From jazz to experimental sounds and psychobilly, you can find what you are looking for almost any night of the week. International names play the Prince Bandroom (see p017), and famed rock haunts are The Tote (71 Johnston Street, T 9419 5320), where there's a sticky carpet and fine beer garden, and Brunswick upstart Howler (see p042). More subdued are Bennetts Lane Jazz Club (25 Bennetts Lane, T 9663 2856) and the Paris Cat (6 Goldie Place, T 9642 4711). Check the listings in *The Age* on Fridays.
For full addresses, see Resources.

Vue de Monde

Chef Shannon Bennett's French-inspired food has always been a showstopper, but when Vue de Monde moved to the 55th floor of The Rialto building (see p025) in 2011, it gained a backdrop to match. Architects Elenberg Fraser used the city's environment – the Yarra, billabongs and native fauna – as a reference. Tables are covered in stretched kangaroo leather and Emma Lashmar's tiny light sculptures are inspired by fireflies. The Gastronomes menu is a 10-course extravaganza of local produce featuring Flinders Island lamb, marron and smoked eel. The entrance to the restaurant and the neighbouring Lui Bar is through the wine cellar, while views stretch as far as the Dandenongs Ranges and Mornington Peninsula (see p098). *Level 55, 525 Collins Street, T 9691 3888, www.vuedemonde.com.au*

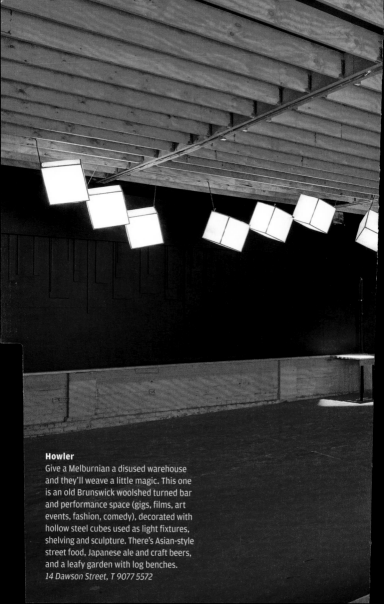

Howler

Give a Melburnian a disused warehouse and they'll weave a little magic. This one is an old Brunswick woolshed turned bar and performance space (gigs, films, art events, fashion, comedy), decorated with hollow steel cubes used as light fixtures, shelving and sculpture. There's Asian-style street food, Japanese ale and craft beers, and a leafy garden with log benches.

14 Dawson Street, T 9077 5572

Bar Ampére

This drinking den is tucked beneath the arches along Russell Place, squatting atop a heritage electricity substation. Designer Donna Brzezinski of architects BG has taken that as inspiration in the industrial front section, where there's a vintage circuit breaker, switches and gauges, and a custom-made Sputnik light. Head past the bathroom, however, to enter another world – the Swamp Room (above) – that wouldn't look out of place in a Louisiana backwater. Fairy lights barely cast a glow and the bar is fashioned from an old piano. Alcohol is taken seriously here (aperitifs and digestifs are a signature) and the tasty morsels from the kitchen keep on coming until 3am. A secret back door leads to sister venue Gin Palace (see p040).
16 Russell Place, T 9663 7557,
www.barampere.com

Cookie

Big, brash and a lot of fun, this beer hall and casual dining hangout is the perfect place to eat and drink at almost any time of day. The fiery Thai food is outrageously good, the peppered pork sticks wrapped in betel leaves are a favourite, and it has acquired some high-profile fans, such as chef Anthony Bourdain. The bistro-style space is defined by a surreal black-and-white collage/mural on one wall, and although it's a cavernous venue, it is so popular you'll often have to wait to be seated. Despite being a long-standing member of the Melbourne scene, Cookie's encyclopaedic drinks list still attracts a mixed crowd of suits and hipsters. Take someone special late in the afternoon and snare a table on the tiny balcony. *Level 1, 252 Swanston Street, T 9663 7660, www.cookie.net.au*

MoVida

Barcelona-born, Melbourne-raised Frank Camorra serves up exceptional food at his tiny unpretentious tapas and wine bar. You often see other chefs here on their days off, tucking into modern interpretations of traditional Spanish small plates at the high tables by the bar. There's also a more conventional dining area if you prefer. We were taken by the *anchoa* (anchovy with smoked tomato sorbet on toasted bread) and duck liver parfait with Pedro Ximenez foam. Its success resulted in the opening of MoVida Next Door (164 Flinders Street), as well as MoVida Aqui (500 Bourke Street), which has Paco's Tacos on its terrace. Take a sunny lunchtime, a fistful of soft-shell tacos, an icy margarita and a communal sombrero and kiss the afternoon goodbye.
1 Hosier Lane, T 9663 3038,
www.movida.com.au

Gingerboy

Chef Teage Ezard became fascinated with street food when working in Hong Kong and decided to open a more relaxed affair than his Asian-influenced fine-diner, Ezard (T 9639 6811). The result is Gingerboy, which serves hawker-style dishes that are meant to be shared. In a small space designed by Elenberg Fraser, walls are lined with black lacquered bamboo and studded with lights, and a tasselled red chandelier dominates the room. We keep coming back for the 'son in law' starter (deep-fried hard-boiled eggs accompanied by chilli jam), the red duck-leg curry with shallots, Thai basil and coconut cream, and ox cheek and sweet potato rendang. After you've eaten, ascend to the jewellery-box cocktail bar, Gingerboy Upstairs.
27-29 Crossley Street, T 9662 4200, www.gingerboy.com.au

Kumo Izakaya

Once a wasteland, this patch of Brunswick East has been resuscitated. Leading the charge were Joseph and Natalie Abboud with their winning Middle Eastern eaterie Rumi (T 9388 8255) and not far behind was Andre Bishop, who set up this Japanese-style gastropub in a former bank. With the help of designer Victor Isobe and artisan builder Bryce Ritchie, Bishop has created a unique space using recycled wood and ironwork. An 8m communal table lit by reading lamps provides a centrepiece and is ringed by intimate booths. Female chefs Akimi Iguchi and Eriko Hamabe create crowd-pleasing small dishes like pan-fried pork gyoza, chicken-skin crackers and kingfish sashimi. Afterwards, there are 70 sakes to sample on the mezzanine level.
152 Lygon Street, T 9388 1505,
www.kumoizakaya.com.au

Siglo

Climb the stairs past the leather couches and old-school ambience of the Melbourne Supper Club (T 9654 6300) to the top-floor Siglo. Since smokers have been banished outdoors, the number of rooftop bars in Melbourne has increased exponentially, and this is one of the finest. An awning stretches over part of the terrace, where wicker chairs surround white-clothed tables. Parliament House is across the street and the Princess Theatre to one side, so it's a lovely setting. There is a choice of Old World wines, beers and cocktails, served by uber-cool staff, but the speciality is cognac and cigars, perfect for ending a night out on the town. Another popular rooftop hangout is the surreal Madame Brussels (T 9662 2775), where Astroturf and plus fours reign supreme.
161 Spring Street, T 9654 6631

Moon Under Water

Chef Andrew McConnell can do little wrong. First, he opened the acclaimed Cutler & Co (T 9419 4888), then, in 2012, took over a local pub, the Builders Arms (T 9417 7700), and transformed it into a culinary hotspot. He has now launched the refined Moon Under Water within the same building. Projects of Imagination have created an all-white space, from the floorboards to the ceiling and the wall of cabinets, contrasted by classic bentwood chairs. Head chef Josh Murphy oversees the set A$75 four-course seasonal menu that features dishes like raw snapper with lovage and dry-aged duck with Cumberland sauce. Alternatively, head into the city to sample McConnell's Cumulus Inc (T 9650 1445) and Supernormal in Flinders Lane. *211 Gertrude Street, T 9417 7700, www.buildersarmshotel.com.au*

New Guernica

Round every corner in this bar designed by co-owner and creative director Kyle Bush, there's something else to catch the eye. Off the main dancefloor, called the Village Square (opposite), are gazebos, nooks and themed rooms (many for hire), including the eponymous Guernica (above), complete with a version of the painting, all meant to invoke a fantasy atmosphere far removed from the bustle of the CBD outside. The late-night spot (it's open until 5am Thursday to Saturday) has various incarnations as the night progresses: it's a casual hangout with great drink deals until 10pm, when DJs (often visiting big names) start to drop the tunes. Downstairs is the equally quirky bar/eaterie Chuckle Park, inspired by holiday caravans.
*Level 2, 322 Little Collins Street,
T 9650 4494, www.newguernica.com.au*

Mr Tulk

There is nothing quiet about the State
Library café, which is named after the
first chief librarian. Located in a grand
room decorated with a mural, it serves
up sardines with salsa verde; pâté with
gherkins on crostini; coffee and cake.
Anglepoise lamps over a central bench
will take you right back to college.
328 Swanston Street, T 8660 5700,
www.slv.vic.gov.au

Seamstress

This former garment factory and brothel has a lot of atmosphere and charm. Rickety wooden staircases lead to various levels, walls are exposed brick, cheongsam hang from the ceilings, and deft touches, such as the angular hardwood blocks of the upstairs bar, add a contemporary edge. The market-dependent menu comprises European takes on pan-Asian dishes such as crispy soft-shell crab with apple and wombok salad, and honey soy braised Wagyu shin with vanilla parsnip purée. Everything is served in either small, medium or large portions. The downstairs watering hole, Sweatshop, has deep-red lighting, scrawled-upon walls and furniture built from caterpillar pallets, and serves excellent cocktails, whisky and craft beer.
113 Lonsdale Street, T 9663 6363, www.seamstress.com.au

Chin Chin

A success since opening in 2011, this funky Thai joint, which is leading the charge towards a more casual inner-city dining scene, hasn't slowed down. Its close-together tables, soaring arched windows, graphic posters and pink neon rabbit are the work of the ubiquitous Projects of Imagination. Chef Benjamin Cooper's food, delivered from the open kitchen, packs a spicy punch. There are a few don't-miss dishes, including crispy barramundi with apple and caramelised pork, and the oyster omelette with chilli and garlic. You can't reserve a table and the wait might be up to two hours, but that doesn't deter the hordes, who happily pass the time in the subterranean GoGo Bar with punch made from plum wine and lychee cocktails.
125 Flinders Lane, T 8663 2000,
www.chinchinrestaurant.com.au

New Gold Mountain

Push through an unassuming door in one of the laneways and follow the steps up to find a sophisticated oriental room with low stools and jade tones. Up another set of stairs is a mini-labyrinth of sexy private rooms (above) separated by laser-cut panels. Fabric installations and Chinese lanterns hang from the ceiling and red patterned wallpaper matches the seating. An eclectic mix of tracks plays softly and there's an extensive range of spirits and cocktails, including the option of matching drinks to sweets from patisserie LuxBite (T 9867 5888). Open until 3am (5am on Fridays and Saturdays), this is the place for deep conversations. New Gold Mountain was the name Chinese immigrants gave each new mine during the gold-rush era. *Levels 1 & 2, 21 Liverpool Street, T 9650 8859, www.newgoldmountain.org*

Spice Market

This subterranean club beneath the Grand Hyatt takes its inspiration from the ancient spice route. The Buchan Group's design incorporates Middle Eastern antiques, a Sri Lankan temple turned seating area, velvet ottomans and birdcages hanging from the ceiling. The Belle Epoque Lounge is the most lavish of the private rooms, hosting up to 14 in a setting that brings to mind the inside of a genie bottle. The atmosphere tends to be subdued until DJs crank it up at 10pm with a soundtrack of house and cool grooves. The signature cocktail is the sweet and potent Turkish Delight martini, and there's a selection of champagne. This is one of the few venues in Melbourne with a dress code; guys must wear collared shirts and proper shoes. *Beaney Lane, Off Russell Street, T 9660 3777, www.spicemarket.net.au*

Hihou

Book ahead, buzz the intercom and climb the stairs to this Japanese lounge designed by John Denton of architects DCM, and run by the owners of hip Izakaya Den (T 9654 2977). A striking timber-batten light fitting mirrors the bar, but the prime position is to be stretched out on the wide banquettes (pictured), sipping a Negro-kan (plum-infused gin, umeshu and Campari).
Level 1, 1 Flinders Lane, T 9654 5465

INSIDER'S GUIDE

KIRRA JAMISON, ARTIST

Australian artist Kirra Jamison (www.kirrajamison.com) settled in Melbourne in 2008 and lives above her studio in an old Northcote factory. 'It's a creative neighbourhood, and my building is full of artists, designers and photographers,' she says. In the morning she makes tracks to Everyday Coffee (33 Johnston Street, T 9973 4159), before a workout at One Hot Yoga (36 River Street, T 040 910 3674). If she has free time, she checks out the contemporary art scene at nearby KalimanRawlins (9 Ellis Street, T 9826 2470), or Utopian Slumps (33 Guildford Lane, T 9077 9918) in the city.

Living in the inner-north means Jamison has plenty of going-out options. 'Long Play (318 St Georges Road, T 040 015 5891) in Fitzroy is my local wine bar and I never regret a trip there. Rum dive Bar Económico (438 Church Street, T 9428 0055) in Richmond is also lots of fun.' For dinner she recommends The Town Mouse Bar & Restaurant (312 Drummond Street, T 9347 3312) for its 'amazing food and casual vibe'. A Latin American trend is sweeping the city; Jamison is a fan of Colombian café Sonido! (69 Gertrude Street) and Los Hermanos (339 Victoria Street, T 9939 3661) in Brunswick, which serves tacos until late. At weekends she likes to cycle along Merri Creek or the Yarra, often to the serene gardens of Abbotsford Convent (1 St Heliers Street, T 9415 3600): 'On balmy summer nights, the Friday supper market and open-air cinema are lovely.' *For full addresses, see Resources.*

ARCHITOUR

A GUIDE TO MELBOURNE'S ICONIC BUILDINGS

Since the early 1990s, Melbourne has undergone an architectural renaissance. New public arts buildings have flourished, and the standards of its residential and commercial developments are the highest in Australia. Local firms – Denton Corker Marshall, Wood/ Marsh, Fender Katsalidis, John Wardle, ARM – are leading the way. Many of the highlights featured here, including ACCA (opposite), the Melbourne Museum (see p068) and Heide Museum of Modern Art (see p072), offer far more than just architectural splendour. Educational institutions are strongly represented too, but then this is a city in which one of the universities, RMIT, employs an Innovation Professor of Architecture. If you visit the Centre for Ideas (see p078) at the Victorian College of the Arts, you should view the aptly theatrical design of its School of Performing Arts (28 Dodds Street, T 9035 9299), by Edmond and Corrigan.

This being Melbourne, there are hidden gems – seek out the abstract shapes and complex geometry of McBride Charles Ryan's Monaco House (22 Ridgway Place), tucked into a tiny 6m by 17m plot in the lanes, and pick up a coffee in Liaison (T 9663 3225) on the ground floor. Much of the domestic architecture is also highly impressive. Sean Godsell's 1997 Kew House (8 Hodgson Street) and Robin Boyd's former family home at 290 Walsh Street, which he designed in 1958, are both visible from the street.

For full addresses, see Resources.

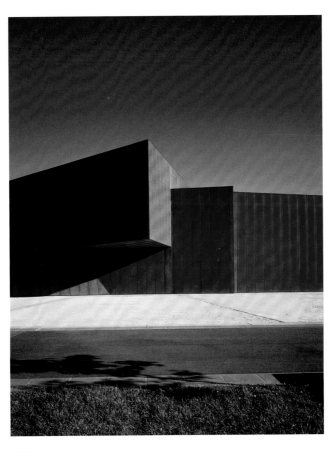

ACCA

Opened in 2002, the Australian Centre for Contemporary Art (ACCA) is a very urban building, between a tangle of roads, train lines and warehouses, yet it resembles the large, rusting agricultural sheds seen in the bush. Architects Roger Wood and Randal Marsh said they wanted to create 'a sculpture in which to show art' and the abstract steel exterior is in stark contrast to the four white-walled gallery spaces as well as the glass foyer, which is accessed by the structure's only obvious opening. ACCA shows work by international and Australian contemporary artists, such as Barbara Kruger, Callum Morton and Gillian Wearing, and is the only major gallery in the country focused on commissioning rather than collecting significant works. *111 Sturt Street, T 9697 9999, www.accaonline.org.au*

MTC and Recital Centre

Designed by architects Ashton Raggatt McDougall, this complex added four performance spaces to the Southbank Cultural Precinct when it opened in 2009. The HQ for Melbourne Theatre Company (MTC; T 8688 0800) has a monochrome interior and a black glass facade fronted by geometric steel tubing that lights up after dark to great 3D effect. Next door, the Recital Centre (T 9699 3333) boasts a huge honeycombed window, and the 1,000-seat Elisabeth Murdoch Hall is lined with routed plywood panels that are visually and acoustically arresting. ARM, in collaboration with architect Peter Elliott, also redeveloped Hamer Hall for 2013 and in the process crucially connected the cultural centre to the river via a terrace and promenade.

140 Southbank Boulevard; 31 Sturt Street

Melbourne Museum

When architects Denton Corker Marshall were commissioned to build the city's museum, they had to somehow contend with its neighbour, the truly magnificent Rundbogenstil-esque Royal Exhibition Building (Carlton Gardens). Designed by Joseph Reed in 1880 for the International Exhibition, and one of the only buildings of its kind left in the world, the Great Hall is still used for its original purpose. It was given a UNESCO World Heritage listing in 2004. Melbourne Museum, which opened in 2000, is located on a slightly raised greenfield site and has all the elements of a DCM design: primary colours, tilted blocks, roof blades over the facade and boxes that house separate elements, such as Bunjilaka, the Aboriginal Cultural Centre. *11 Nicholson Street, T 131 102, www.museumvictoria.com.au*

Monash City Council

One of just four buildings in Melbourne by the great Harry Seidler, this government office in Glen Waverley sits on beautiful sloping parkland. The most outstanding aspect is the semicircular skylight vault over a chamber that otherwise has no windows. The 1984 structure comprises two wings: one containing the council chambers, mayor's office and function and meeting spaces; the other housing the administrative departments. The two are linked by a high atrium foyer, which is used for events, and a suspended bridge across the entrance. Seidler aficionados should also check out Shell House (1 Spring Street), the Karralyka Centre (Mines Road) in Ringwood and the Monash Gallery of Art (T 8544 0500) in Wheelers Hill.
293 Springvale Road, T 9518 3555, www.monash.vic.gov.au

Webb Bridge
As much sculpture as pedestrian access, this 145m-long bridge, a collaboration between Denton Corker Marshall, artist Robert Owen and Arup, links Docklands and Southbank across the Yarra. Owen used laser-cut steel lattice to represent the eel traps used by Aborigines who had once lived in the area. It was floated into position on a high tide in 2003.
Parallel to Charles Grimes Bridge Road

Heide Museum of Modern Art

This cultural complex in Bulleen consists of four buildings: the original weatherboard farmhouse; Heide II, a 1965 modernist masterpiece by David McGlashan; Heide III (pictured), a 2006 gallery by O'Connor + Houle that houses a permanent art collection; and the Sidney Myer Education Centre. The property was bought in 1934 by John and Sunday Reed, who opened their modest home to artists of the calibre of Sidney Nolan, Albert Tucker and Joy Hester, making Heide one of the most significant addresses in the history of Australian art. Today, tour the museums, sculpture park and grounds, where chef Shannon Bennett, who owns the on-site Café Vue Heide (T 9852 2346), grows produce in the Reeds' old kitchen garden. *7 Templestowe Road, T 9850 1500, www.heide.com.au*

Pixel Building

It's hard to miss Studio 505's office block, which opened in 2010 on a 250 sq m patch of the old Carlton & United Breweries site. Covered in recycled coloured panels, it has been likened to a jester's cloak. Some accuse it of being garish, yet the bright protrusions are not simply attention-grabbing – it is the first carbon-neutral office building in Australia and the facade allows 100 per cent daylight penetration while protecting workers from direct sun and glare. On top of the four storeys is a rooftop garden with wind turbines and solar panels. Methane is extracted from black waste to heat water, ledges at each level create shading, hold gardens and transport grey water for treatment, and vacuum toilets are installed throughout. Environmental concerns are even at the very core – the concrete used creates 60 per cent less carbon during manufacture.
205 Queensberry Street

Lyon Housemuseum

Corbett and Yueji Lyon not only designed their own home, but have opened it up as a public gallery showing an impressive collection of contemporary art. On display are paintings, sculpture, installations and video art by Australians including Patricia Piccinini, Shaun Gladwell and Howard Arkley. The ground floor connects with a set of courtyards and sculpture gardens, whereas upstairs is more enclosed, its rooms leading off a balconied atrium. The distinctive exterior is clad in grey zinc. As visitors wander through the house, the hosts go about their everyday business; it's not unusual to see the children doing their homework. Understandably, the museum, located in suburban Kew, only opens on specific days. Book in advance. *219 Cotham Road, T 9817 2300, www.lyonhousemuseum.com.au*

Centre for Ideas
Paul Minifie and Fiona Nixon's futuristic
2004 annexe to the Victorian College of
the Arts boasts a facade of shimmering
shallow cones, which culminate either in
windows or reflective domes. Inspired by
a Voronoi tessellation, the articulation is
superb, and apt for a centre that explores
the links between art and philosophy.
234 St Kilda Road, T 9685 9343,
www.vca.unimelb.edu.au/cfi

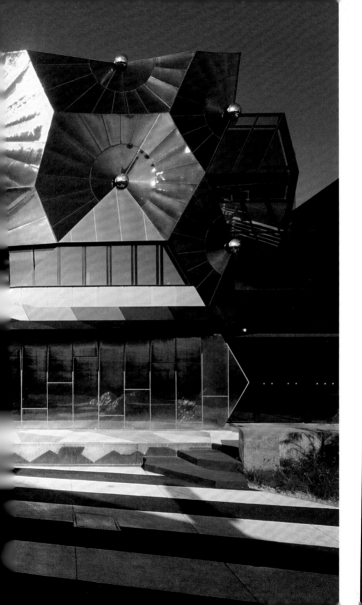

SHOPPING

THE BEST RETAIL THERAPY AND WHAT TO BUY

Melbourne has its fair share of soulless suburban mega-malls, but it is also a city of quirky village-style high streets and independent retailers. Upmarket and genteel Armadale (7km south-east of the CBD) has more than 200 boutique premises, including antiques centres, bookstores and the ateliers and showrooms of Australian designers such as Camilla and Marc (1067 High Street, T 9804 3111) and Lee Mathews (1059 High Street, T 9822 8174).

We suggest you head to the suburbs of the inner north as well. For handmade accessories, try Five Boroughs (345 Lygon Street, T 9388 1618) or browse the eclectic selection of books, stationery, music and presents at Brunswick Bound (361 Sydney Road, T 9381 4019). This area is also home to great Middle Eastern food, funky cafés and cool bars, and is more of a 'local' haunt than the popular areas of Fitzroy and St Kilda. Nearby Northcote is a great spot to stroll with your credit card. Visit Obüs (285 High Street, T 9482 3330) for Kylie Zerbst's bold, quirky, global-inspired fashion, all of which is manufactured locally, and Hummingbird 60 (244 High Street, T 9486 6778) for Australian clothing, jewellery and gifts.

On the weekend, go outdoors, to The Rose St Artists' Market (60 Rose Street, T 9419 5529), which sells art, fashion and bibelots, while more than 150 artisans set up on Sundays at The Esplanade Market (Upper Esplanade, T 9209 6634) by the water in St Kilda. *For full addresses, see Resources.*

Third Drawer Down

Despite its diminutive size, this self-titled Museum of Art Souvenirs stocks a huge range of covetable pieces, curated by a company that started out by producing limited-edition artist-designed tea towels. These are still available to buy along with a variety of lovingly selected products such as interior design objects, bedlinen, toys, stationery and all manner of things you simply must have but can't work out why.

On a recent visit, we left with a Tom Dixon marble spice grinder, edible chalk (you never know when you'll need a writing utensil that doubles as a snack) and David Shrigley guitar picks. New York retailer Kiosk has also set up here, selling eclectic items including an Italian tape dispenser, leather snowshoes and a mushroom knife.
93 George Street, T 9534 4088,
www.thirddrawerdown.com

Double Monk

Brothers Chris and Nick Schaerf injected some glamour into the men's scene with this deluxe shoe salon designed by Antony Martin of architects MRTN. Stained timber shelving lined with pool-table felt, rolling ladders, salvaged oak parquet flooring, a pressed metal ceiling, leather club chairs and taxidermy creates an ambience that invites customers to kick off and kick back. It's all about handmade English shoes here, by John Lobb, George Cleverley, Edward Green and Crockett & Jones, and there's a selection of gents' accessories including umbrellas, ties, glasses, pocket squares and leather goods. Take the edge off at the in-store whisky bar; try one of the rarer varieties, perhaps the Sullivans Cove single cask from Tasmania, if in stock. *53 Smith Street, T 9417 3335, www.doublemonk.com*

Green With Envy

Unlike the northern suburbs where indie and vintage reign, Chapel Street in South Yarra showcases a sleeker style. For some of Australia's finest fashion, alongside innovative international acts, head to the flagship Green With Envy store. Dion Lee, Ginger & Smart, Sass & Bide and Josh Goot hang next to Céline, Helmut Lang and Miu Miu. There are also high-end shoes, bags and accessories, including Karen Walker Eyewear. David Hicks' sleek, high-gloss design – glass and marble feature strongly – is the ideal minimal backdrop. There's another Green With Envy outpost in Flinders Lane, which is home to other top designers including Gorman (T 9826 4556), who, in a city that adores its basic black, strikes out with colour and pattern. *517 Chapel Street, T 180 067 4047, www.greenwithenvy.com.au*

Leif

Sydney-based skincare company Leif uses botanical extracts blended with essential oils to create its small but perfectly formed product line. Indigenous ingredients such as wild rosella, alpine pepper, desert lime, lemon myrtle and eucalyptus are married with vanilla, sandalwood and orange to create its body balm, hand wash, hand balm and body cleanser (above), A$19.95. They are all free from paraben, alcohol, synthetic fragrances and artificial colours, and come in stylish recyclable packaging by design company Container. Buy them at Mr Darcy (T 9682 7110) and A Quirk of Fate (T 9486 7929) or online. Find more Australian cosmetics at Aesop, the local brand gone global, which has distinctive typographical labelling. Its stores across the city are all designed by architects.
www.leifskincare.com

Captains of Industry

This suave gentlemen's outfitter, café and barber specialises in bespoke kangaroo leather footwear from bootmaker Theo Hassett and custom-hemmed Japanese selvedge denim by RHD. The fit-out of the warehouse space, located up a flight of creaky stairs on the first floor of an old watchmakers' factory overlooking the historic GPO Building, is low-key; vintage-style pieces have come from auction rooms or were family heirlooms. Stop to grab some lunch in the café that overlooks Elizabeth Street – the steak sandwich with onion jam is a popular choice but there are excellent salads, own-brand coffee and a select wine list – or get a sharp trim or shave from Sam Fordyce; the grooming products are for sale.
Level 1, 2 Somerset Place, T 9670 4405, www.captainsofindustry.com.au

Claude Maus

Stylish and understated, this unisex fashion label is quintessentially Melbourne and a favourite of bands such as Cut Copy. Former artist and graphic designer Rob Maniscalco layers together dark themes and a sombre palette. Particularly popular are the leather pieces central to the winter collections and the no-nonsense denim range. Maniscalco and architects Herbert & Mason collaborated on the interior of this heritage-listed building, which features recycled timber, eye-catching macramé hangings and a handmade wooden light by David Noonan. Imported accessories and shoes are on sale too. Also well worth a browse is another local brand, Alpha60 (T 9663 3002), created by siblings Alex and Georgie Cleary, nearby on Flinders Lane. *19 Manchester Lane, T 9654 9844, www.claudemaus.com*

SPORTS AND SPAS

WORK OUT, CHILL OUT OR JUST WATCH

Don't roll your eyes when a local starts talking about the summer's Test series or the fortunes of their footy team. Melburnians take their sport seriously, and you'll be expected to as well. Aussie Rules football (or AFL) was born here and is a religion. The season takes place in winter and games are played at the MCG (see p012). Other major draws are the Spring Racing Carnival and Melbourne Cup (November), the Open tennis (January) and the Grand Prix (March).

Aussies are an active lot and it's easy to stay in shape. Melbourne Sports & Aquatic Centre (375 Albert Road, T 9926 1555) has a fitness centre and outdoor pools, plus squash, badminton and basketball courts. Also in Albert Park, The Boatyard (3 Aquatic Drive, T 9699 3444) hires out vessels to sail on the lake, while Kayak Melbourne (Shed 2, North Wharf Road, T 041 810 6427) runs tours of the Yarra, embarking from Docklands. Or jog along The Tan, a 3.8km path around the Botanic Gardens – the lap record stands at 10 minutes 12 seconds. In the heat, the draw of Medibank Icehouse (105 Pearl River Road, T 130 075 6699) may be more appealing. You can skate or cheer on the Mustangs hockey team (April to September).

For pampering, the luxurious Chuan Spa (Level 9, 1 Southgate Avenue, T 8696 8111) at The Langham (see p016) merges holistic Eastern practices with modern techniques, while the Aurora Spa (T 9536 1130) at The Prince (see p017) is also recommended. *For full addresses, see Resources.*

Isika Day Spa

This spa is situated high above the city on the 27th floor of the Crown Metropol hotel (see p024). There are 10 treatment rooms (including two for couples) decorated in neutral tones and shrouded in linen, each offering a selection of music channels. Therapists perform massage miracles (go for the 90-minute Fusion Stone Massage) and facials using Aveda products. There's a hair and nail salon, and even treatments for the Aussie man, but what excites us most are the facilities. Changing rooms have vitality pools, steam rooms and ice showers but the standout feature is the panorama from the infinity pool and sun deck (overleaf). For a complete overhaul, check into an Isika Luxe room on the 26th floor. Open until 8pm (pool and gym, 9pm). *Crown Metropol, 8 Whiteman Street, T 9292 8327, www.crownmetropol.com.au*

Infinity pool, Isika Day Spa

Hardrock CBD

Even beginners should be able to scale the heights at this climbing gym. The rendered concrete wall is 18m at its apex but, given it starts one storey up, the CBD views from the top through the full-length glass wall are extraordinary. The entry fee allows all-day access but don't count on spending too many hours here – this is an intense full-body workout. Normally you'd need a partner, but the venue has four auto-belay walls (ring for availability), a device that 'holds' the rope, allowing you to climb alone, and you can hire a harness and shoes, as well as a private instructor. Across the road, the red-brick Melbourne City Baths (T 9663 5888) were designed by JJ Clark and opened in 1904. Facilities include a pool, spa, sauna and gym. *501 Swanston Street, T 9631 5300, www.hardrock.com.au*

Onsen Ma

Amid the lively nightlife of the laneways, this Japanese bathhouse is a den of calm. Andrea Borazio transformed a disused space, with the help of restaurant designer Victor Isobe, using painted plywood walls, glazed tiles and decorative pieces such as silk wedding kimonos, and much of the art on display was painted by receptionist Keiko Murakami. In separate bathing areas for men and women (above), mineral-rich water is kept at 38°C to 40°C; there's also a private spa with steam room for couples and families. The etiquette is to soak for 10 to 15 minutes, then take a sauna before returning to the baths (A$30 for an hour). Onsen Ma specialises in shiatsu massage and has a sunny outdoor deck on which you can chat afterwards over green tea.
Level 1, 12-18 Meyers Place, T 9663 8777, www.onsenma.com.au

AAMI Park

In response to the increase in popularity of other football codes aside from AFL, which is played on an oval pitch, this stadium, which has a rectangular field and a seating capacity of more than 30,000, opened in 2010. It's adjacent to the MCG (see p012), the Olympic Park and the Rod Laver Arena in the sports precinct. Designed by Cox Architecture, AAMI Park has a geodesic roof and was colloquially known as the Bubble Dome while being built. Now often referred to as the Rectangular Stadium, it is home to the rugby league team Storm; the Rebels, who entered the Super 15 rugby union competition in 2011; and a pair of rather optimistically named A-League soccer teams, Victory and Heart. *Olympic Boulevard, T 9286 1600, www.aamipark.com.au*

ESCAPES

WHERE TO GO IF YOU WANT TO LEAVE TOWN

It is possible to head in almost any direction from Melbourne and find thriving country towns, vineyards and staggeringly beautiful coast. The Great Ocean Road stretches almost as far as the South Australian border. It follows the Shipwreck Coast (it's called that for good reason), passing famous Bells Beach, the Twelve Apostles, the fashionable resort of Lorne and the fishing village of Apollo Bay. Another pristine town, Port Fairy, has the boutique hotel Drift House (opposite) and a number of surfing beaches. Closer are the stalwarts of the Mornington Peninsula, including Sorrento, Portsea and Flinders (see p098), from where you can sail, or drive to the rolling vineyards, known for their excellent pinot noir.

It's also a short jaunt to the wineries of the Yarra Valley. The main town, Healesville, is 45 minutes away – here, try the cellar at Innocent Bystander (336 Maroondah Highway, T 5962 6111) as well as the wood-fired pizza. One of the best vineyards is Yering Station (38 Melba Highway, Yarra Glen, T 9730 0100), which has a restaurant and art gallery. Continue north-east to the gold-rush town of Beechworth (three hours from Melbourne), which is now reinvented as a foodie's paradise. In the old Bank of Australasia, chef Michael Ryan runs Provenance (86 Ford Street, T 5728 1786), where exquisite cuisine with Japanese influences is served. Stay in one of the four Asian-inspired suites in the carriage house. *For full addresses, see Resources.*

Drift House, Port Fairy

Stretching 243km west from Torquay to Allansford, near Warrnambool, the Great Ocean Road is, in fact, the world's largest war memorial, built from 1919 to 1932 by returned soldiers and dedicated to those who died in WWI. Take time out to explore the Great Otway Ranges and the beautiful coastline, and watch the sun rise over the Twelve Apostles rock stacks. Just beyond the road's end is Port Fairy, a fishing village at the mouth of the Moyne River with more than 50 historic buildings, including this bluestone residence from 1875. Architects Multiplicity have added a contemporary extension and it is now a luxe retreat with four individual suites featuring bespoke art and furniture. We like Suite 1 (above), which has a fireplace and wide veranda. *98 Gipps Street, T 043 996 9282, www.drifthouse.com.au*

Flinders Hotel, Flinders

The Mornington Peninsula is becoming a gourmet destination as visitors to the region's 170-plus vineyards look to dine on fare the equal of its chardonnay and pinot. At its south-eastern tip, just over an hour's drive from the city, the revamped Flinders Hotel is now a welcome presence on the scene. Architects Rothe Lowman added 40 modern rooms and suites, most with patios or balconies, and refurbished the old pub into two dining areas. The Deck is casual, serving salt-and-pepper squid and grilled quail, while Terminus (opposite) is a fine-diner where chef Pierre Khodja weaves his French-meets-North African magic. During the day, stroll the secluded beaches, go dolphin-watching or relax at Peninsula Hot Springs (T 5950 8777). *Cook Street/Wood Street, T 5989 0201, www.flindershotel.com.au*

Zealandia, Portsea

Set in Portsea, a resort on Mornington Peninsula that's favoured by well-to-do Melburnians, Zealandia is about one and a half hour's drive from the city. The classic 1950s beach house has been restored right down to the blue mosaic swimming pool and original period furniture. Large windows look out on to tranquil gardens, there's an extensive deck for entertaining under a cantilevered roof, as well as an open fireplace and modern kitchen and bathroom facilities. There are three big bedrooms plus additional sleeping space in the second living area, making it the perfect destination for a group. It's all about unwinding here – you can walk to either of the two beaches, hire a yacht for a day's sailing and enjoy a sunset dinner overlooking the sea from the bistro at Portsea Hotel (T 5984 2213). *T 9650 2523, www.zealandia.com.au*

Lake House, Daylesford

Once at the centre of Victoria's gold rush, Daylesford, about an 80-minute journey from Melbourne, is better known today as a spa town. The stylish and relaxing Lake House has 35 rooms and suites set alongside the Salus Spa, which features its own bottled water, and treatment rooms in treehouses. Lake House is also famous for its restaurant, where chef Alla Wolf-Tasker creates dishes of such excellence that this is regarded as one of the finest eateries in Australia. Also in the grounds is a self-contained two-bed country house known as The Retreat. The local area has a flourishing arts scene, good golf courses and the historic Botanic Gardens, where Wolf-Tasker runs the café and produce store Wombat Hill House.

King Street, T 5348 3329,
www.lakehouse.com.au

Boyd Baker House, Bacchus Marsh

In isolated bushland less than an hour from Melbourne is one of Australia's most important modernist houses, which, since 2007, has been available to rent. Designed by Robin Boyd, considered to be one of Australia's leading architects and social commentators, the six-bedroom Baker House was completed in 1966. Arranged around a central courtyard, the house features curved internal walls of locally hewn sandstone. The glass facades of the outer rooms give the feeling of actually living out in the bush. The smaller Dower House, also by Robin Boyd, and a library designed by Sir Roy Grounds in 1977, are part of the complex. Surrounded by 400 hectares of reserve, this is a truly luxurious escape into the Australian wilderness. *Long Forest Road, T 8508 6444, www.boydbakerhouse.com.au*

NOTES
SKETCHES AND MEMOS

RESOURCES

CITY GUIDE DIRECTORY

A

A Quirk of Fate 085
289 High Street
Northcote
T 9486 7929
www.aquirkoffate.com

AAMI Park 094
Olympic Boulevard
T 9286 1600
www.aamipark.com.au

Abbotsford Convent 062
1 St Heliers Street
T 9415 3600
www.abbotsfordconvent.com.au

ACCA 065
111 Sturt Street
T 9697 9999
www.accaonline.org.au

Acland St Cantina 017
The Prince
2 Acland Street
T 9536 1175
www.aclandstcantina.com.au

Alpha60 087
201 Flinders Lane
T 9663 3002
www.alpha60.com.au

Amor y Locura 034
77 Gertrude Street
T 9486 0270
www.amorylocura.com

Anna Schwartz Gallery 036
185 Flinders Lane
T 9654 6131
www.annaschwartzgallery.com

Attica 040
74 Glen Eira Road
T 9530 0111
www.attica.com.au

Aurora Spa 088
The Prince
2 Acland Street
T 9536 1130
www.aurorasparetreat.com

B

Bar Ampére 044
16 Russell Place
T 9663 7557
www.barampere.com

Bar Económico 062
438 Church Street
Richmond
T 9428 0055
www.bareconomico.com.au

Bennetts Lane Jazz Club 040
25 Bennetts Lane
T 9663 2856
www.bennettslane.com

The Boatyard 088
3 Aquatic Drive
T 9699 3444
www.theboatyard.com.au

Brunswick Bound 080
361 Sydney Road
Brunswick
T 9381 4019
www.brunswickbound.com.au

Builders Arms Hotel 051
211 Gertrude Street
T 9417 7700
www.buildersarmshotel.com.au

C

Café Vue Heide 072
Heide Museum of Modern Art
7 Templestowe Road
T 9852 2346
www.heide.com.au/cafe-vue-heide

HOTELS

ADDRESSES AND ROOM RATES

The Blackman 016
Room rates:
double, from A$240
452 St Kilda Road
Fawkner Park
T 9039 1444
www.artserieshotels.com.au/blackman

Boyd Baker House 103
Room rates:
double, from A$1,650;
Dower House, from A$1,850
Robin Boyd Baker Compound
Long Forest Road
Bacchus Marsh
T 8508 6444
www.boydbakerhouse.com.au

Brooklyn Arts Hotel 030
Room rates:
double, from A$155;
Green Piano Room, A$245
48-50 George Street
Fitzroy
T 9419 9328
www.brooklynartshotel.com.au

Crown Metropol 024
Room rates:
double, from A$255;
City Luxe King, from A$310;
Loft, from A$605
Level 1
8 Whiteman Street
T 9292 6211
www.crownmetropol.com.au

The Cullen 028
Room rates:
double, from A$220;
Studio Suite, from A$220;
Cullen Suite, from A$330;
Deluxe Balcony, from A$330
164 Commercial Road
T 9098 1555
www.artserieshotels.com.au/cullen

Drift House 097
Room rates:
double, from A$295;
Suite 1, from A$325
98 Gipps Street
Port Fairy
T 043 996 9282
www.drifthouse.com.au

Flinders Hotel 098
Room rates:
double, from A$200
Cook Street/Wood Street
Flinders
T 5989 0201
www.flindershotel.com.au

Grand Hyatt 016
Room rates:
double, from A$275;
Grand View, from A$300
123 Collins Street
T 9657 1234
www.melbourne.grand.hyatt.com

Lake House 102
Room rates:
double, from A$550;
The Retreat, prices on request
King Street
Daylesford
T 5348 3329
www.lakehouse.com.au

The Langham 016
Room rates:
double, from A$370;
Club Terrace, from A$770
1 Southgate Avenue
T 8696 8888
www.melbourne.langhamhotels.com.au

Lyall Hotel and Spa 016
Room rates:
double, from A$735;
Suite 401, from A$1,135
16 Murphy Street
South Yarra
T 9868 8222
www.thelyall.com

Middle Park Hotel 022
Room rates:
double, from A$145;
King Suite, from A$280
102 Canterbury Road
Middle Park
T 9690 1958
www.middleparkhotel.com.au

The Olsen 016
Room rates:
double, from A$240
637-641 Chapel Street
South Yarra
T 9040 1222
www.artserieshotels.com.au/olsen

Ovolo 020
Room rates:
double, from A$220;
Terrace Suite, from A$560;
Penthouse, from A$705
19 Little Bourke Street
T 8692 0777
www.ovolohotels.com

The Prince 017
Room rates:
double, from A$175;
Premier Suite 409, from A$530
2 Acland Street
T 9536 1111
www.theprince.com.au

The Rialto 025
Room rates:
double, from A$265;
Turret Suite, from A$370
495 Collins Street
T 8627 1400
www.ihg.com/hotels

Sofitel 016
Room rates:
double, from A$295
25 Collins Street
T 9653 0000
www.sofitelmelbourne.com.au

Zealandia 100
Room rates:
prices on request
Portsea
T 9650 2523
www.zealandia.com.au

WALLPAPER* CITY GUIDES

Executive Editor
Rachael Moloney

Editor
Jeremy Case
Author
Carrie Hutchinson

Art Editor
Eriko Shimazaki
Designer
Mayumi Hashimoto
Map Illustrator
Russell Bell

Photography Editor
Elisa Merlo
Assistant Photography Editor
Nabil Butt

Chief Sub-Editor
Nick Mee
Sub-Editor
Farah Shafiq

Editorial Assistant
Emilee Jane Tombs

Intern
Blossom Green

Wallpaper* Group Editor-in-Chief
Tony Chambers
Publishing Director
Gord Ray
Managing Editor
Oliver Adamson

Original Design
Loran Stosskopf

Wallpaper* ® is a
registered trademark
of IPC Media Limited

First published 2007
Revised and updated
2011 and 2014

All prices are correct at
the time of going to press,
but are subject to change.

Printed in China

PHAIDON

Phaidon Press Limited
Regent's Wharf
All Saints Street
London N1 9PA

Phaidon Press Inc
65 Bleecker Street
New York, NY 10012

Phaidon® is a registered
trademark of Phaidon
Press Limited

www.phaidon.com

PHOTOGRAPHERS

**Wolfram Janzer/
Artur/VIEW**
Federation Square,
pp014-015

Peter Bennetts
New Gold Mountain, p058

Sean Fennessy
Howler, pp042-043

Trevor Mein
MCG, p012

Mark Munro
Melbourne city view,
inside front cover
The Prince, p017,
pp018-019
Ovolo, p020, p021
CIBI, p033
Tarlo & Graham, p034
Jimmy Grants, p035
Coda, p038, p039
Vue de Monde, p041
Bar Ampére, p044
Kumo Izakaya, pp048-049
New Guernica, p052, p053
Chin Chin, p057
Spice Market, p059
Kirra Jamison, p063
Monash City Council, p069
Pixel Building, pp074-075
Double Monk, pp082-083
Green With Envy, p084
Captains of Industry, p086
Hardrock CBD, p092
Onsen Ma, p093

Dianna Snape
Lyon Housemuseum,
p076, p077

Derek Swalwell
Melbourne Gateway,
pp010-011
Republic Tower, p013
Middle Park
Hotel, pp022-023
Crown Metropol, p024
The Rialto, p025,
pp026-027
The Cullen, p028, p029
Brooklyn Arts
Hotel, pp030-031
Cookie, p045
MoVida, p046
Siglo, p050
Seamstress, p056
ACCA, p065
MTC and Recital
Centre, pp066-067
Melbourne Museum, p068
Heide Museum of Modern
Art, pp072-073
Centre for Ideas,
pp078-079
Third Drawer Down, p081
AAMI Park, pp094-095

Richard Whitbread
Moon Under Water, p051

MELBOURNE

A COLOUR-CODED GUIDE TO THE HOT 'HOODS

CENTRAL BUSINESS DISTRICT
The densely packed CBD buzzes both day and night, alive with shops, restaurants and bars

SOUTHBANK
A giant pleasure palace, five-star hotels and the city's cultural precinct overlook the Yarra

CARLTON
Italian immigrants settled here and excellent trattorias surround the Melbourne Museum

ST KILDA
This laidback suburb, full of bookstores, bars and cafés, runs down to the waterfront

SOUTH YARRA
High-end boutiques, top eateries and lots of verdant space give the district a village feel

COLLINGWOOD/FITZROY
An arty, up-and-coming, bohemian enclave that is home to the Spanish community

For a full description of each neighbourhood, see the Introduction.
Featured venues are colour-coded, according to the district in which they are located.